OFF TO
ANDHRA PRADESH

SONIA MEHTA

PUFFIN BOOKS
An imprint of Penguin Random House

PUFFIN BOOKS

USA | Canada | UK | Ireland | Australia | New Zealand | India | South Africa | China | Singapore

Puffin Books is part of the Penguin Random House group of companies whose addresses can be found at global.penguinrandomhouse.com

Published by Penguin Random House India Pvt. Ltd
4th Floor, Capital Tower 1, MG Road,
Gurugram 122 002, Haryana, India

Penguin
Random House
India

First published in Puffin Books by Penguin Random House India 2018

Picture Credits

P 6: Visakhapatnam (Prawat Thananithaporn/Shutterstock.com); P 9: Paddy fields (© Adityamadhav83 (Own work) [CC BY-SA 3.0 (https://creativecommons.org/licenses/by-sa/3.0)], via Wikimedia Commons); P 12: A fighter plane, Visakhapatnam (tantrik71/Shutterstock.com); P 13: Tirupati temple (CRS PHOTO/Shutterstock.com), Tirupati shrine (CRS PHOTO/Shutterstock.com); Peer darga, Kadapa (© Rajaraman Sundaram [CC BY 3.0 (http://creativecommons.org/licenses/by/3.0)], via Wikimedia Commons); P 14: Life scenes of Buddha, from the 2nd century found in Amaravati, Andhra Pradesh, now exposed in the Indian Museum in Kolkata (Zvonimir Atletic/Shutterstock.com); P 16: Eastern Chalukyan coin (© Classical Numismatic Group, Inc. http://www.cngcoins.com [GFDL (http://www.gnu.org/copyleft/fdl.html), CC-BY-SA-3.0 (http://creativecommons.org/licenses/by-sa/3.0/) or CC BY-SA 2.5 (https://creativecommons.org/licenses/by-sa/2.5)], via Wikimedia Commons); P 20: Villagers in Puttaparthi (gg-foto/Shutterstock.com); P 22: A Haridasu (reddees/Shutterstock.com), A Lambada dancer (reddees/Shutterstock.com); P 23: Cheriyal scroll painting (© Rangan Datta Wiki (Own work) [CC BY-SA 3.0 (https://creativecommons.org/licenses/by-sa/3.0) or GFDL (http://www.gnu.org/copyleft/fdl.html)], via Wikimedia Commons), Cheriyal masks (© Rangan Datta Wiki (Own work) [CC BY-SA 3.0 (https://creativecommons.org/licenses/by-sa/3.0)], via Wikimedia Commons); P 27: Pongal celebrations (reddees/Shutterstock.com); P 33: Lord Venkateshwara (© Kalyan Kanuri (originally posted to Flickr as Lord Venkateswara) [CC BY-SA 2.0 (https://creativecommons.org/licenses/by-sa/2.0)], via Wikimedia Commons); P 34: Aerial view of Srikalahasti (AjayTvm/Shutterstock.com), Kanaka Durga Temple (© Srikar Kashyap (Own work) [CC BY-SA 4.0 (https://creativecommons.org/licenses/by-sa/4.0)], via Wikimedia Commons); P 37: Stone carvings, Amaravthi, India (reddees/Shutterstock.com), Sculpture of Lord Shiva (tantrik71/Shutterstock.com); P 38: Bojjannakonda (© Adityamadhav83 (Own work) [CC BY-SA 3.0 (https://creativecommons.org/licenses/by-sa/3.0)], via Wikimedia Commons); P 39: Nagarjunakonda (© Michael Gunther (Own work) [CC BY-SA 4.0 (https://creativecommons.org/licenses/by-sa/4.0)], via Wikimedia Commons); P 40: Farmer in Andhra Pradesh (reddees/Shutterstock.com); P 41: Man with a herd of cattle (gg-foto/Shutterstock.com); P 45: A typical Andhra meal (© PriyaBooks [CC BY 2.0 (http://creativecommons.org/licenses/by/2.0)], via Wikimedia Commons); P 60: Visakhapatnam (SNEHIT/Shutterstock.com)

The views and opinions expressed in this book are the author's own and the facts are as reported by her, which have been verified to the extent possible, and the publishers are not in any way liable for the same.

The information in this book is based on research from bona fide sites and published books and is true to the best of the author's knowledge at the time of going to print. The author is not responsible for any further changes or developments occurring post the publication of this book. This series is not a comprehensive representation of the states of India but is intended to give children a flavour of the lifestyles and cultures of different states. All illustrations are artistic representations only.

ISBN 9780143440840

Design and layout by Quadrum Solutions Pvt. Ltd
Printed at Repro India Limited

www.penguin.co.in

This is a legitimate digitally printed version of the book and therefore might not have certain extra finishing on the cover.

Hello Kids!

I'm so happy you are reading this book. India is an incredible country and there are lots of things about it that we never get to hear about.

I discovered India because my father was in the Indian army. He was posted to many places all over India—and we dutifully followed him. Can you imagine that by the time I was in the tenth standard, I had changed nine schools? Of course it was hard making new friends almost every year, but the good part was that I got to live in so many places. Right from Kerala, where I was born, to Kashmir, Jhansi, Shillong, Chandigarh, Goa . . . the list is long.

Every time I go to a new place, I feel amazed at how different each state is from the other—and yet, how similar. Did you know that we can see monuments from the Stone Age right here in India? Or that we have more than twenty official languages, and most Indians know three or four on an average? Or even that some of the world's most amazing scientific marvels were invented in India?

Oh, there are many, many, many fun and fantastic things about the states of India, which we simply must get to know.

So get your backpack ready, get set to meet some new friends, and join me on a fun trip as we **DISCOVER INDIA, STATE BY STATE**.

I hope you enjoy reading this book as much as I have enjoyed writing it. I would love to hear from you. So do write to me at sonia.mehta@quadrumltd.com.

Lots of love,
Sonia Aunty

Mishki and Pushka have come to visit Earth from their home planet, Zoomba. They have never seen such an amazing place. Zoomba doesn't have trees and mountains and rivers like Earth does. But the people look exactly the same. When they come to Earth, they meet a sweet old man whom they call Daadu Dolma. Daadu Dolma shows them all the wonderful places in India and tells Mishki and Pushka all about them.

Mishki and Pushka can't believe what they see. They have seen a lot of Earth, but they have never, ever seen a place like India.

They are off to explore India state by state :)

Mishki

Mishki is a curious little girl. She is always asking loads of questions. On her home planet, she is always getting into trouble for poking her nose into things that are not her business.

Pushka

Pushka is Mishki's brother. He loves adventure. He is always ready for a new challenge. Whether it's climbing a mountain, or diving into a cold, cold sea, he is up for it.

Daadu Dolma

Daadu Dolma is a wise old man who has lived on Earth longer than the mountains and the seas. No one knows quite how old he is, but he certainly has been around. He knows everything about everything.

Pushka hasn't slept all night. He's been reading about Andhra Pradesh. 'Daadu, I am really curious about this state,' he says. 'It seems to have a rich history—but is very modern too.'

'You're right,' Daadu agrees. 'That's what makes Andhra Pradesh so special.' 'Let's stop talking and leave right away,' says Mishki, clapping her hands. She loves to visit new places.

'Okay then,' smiles Daadu, 'get your bags ready and let's go.' Mishki and Pushka let out a whoop of delight. They are

OFF TO ANDHRA PRADESH!!!

Land ahoy!

Ah! I can see a little bit of the sea here, Daadu. Can we swim?

You can if you want to. But first, come and see all of Andhra Pradesh. There's so much to do, you might not have much time to swim. Let's get going!

ON THE MAP

To see exactly where Andhra Pradesh is on the map of India, go to

http://www.mapsofindia.com/maps/india/india-political-map.htm

NEIGHBOURING JOY

Andhra Pradesh was once a very large state. Then, just recently, it was divided into two states—Telangana and Andhra Pradesh. This made the state a little smaller, but it still has a lot of lovely neighbours. It is surrounded by Karnataka, Tamil Nadu, Odisha and, of course, Telangana. On its eastern side, it has a long coastline, where the waters of the Bay of Bengal lap its shores.

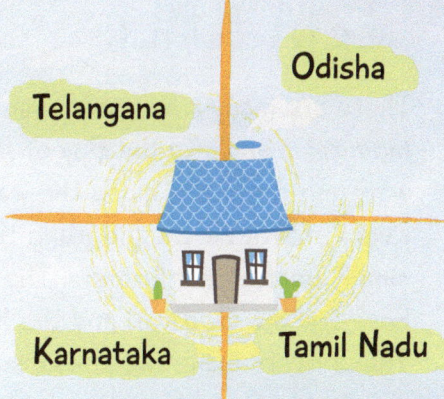

Telangana

Odisha

Karnataka

Tamil Nadu

CAPITAL CRUNCH

We will find out a little later how Telangana became a different state. But what is important to know is that it currently shares its capital with Andhra Pradesh. The lovely old city of Hyderabad is the capital of these two states.

THE LAND TRIO

Andhra Pradesh has three kinds of landforms. The long plains that run along the coast, the Eastern Ghats that stand strong along its western boundary and the large plateau that covers the south-west.

DELTA FORCE

There are many rivers that rush down the mountains and into the Bay of Bengal, watering the plains along the way. These rivers create deltas and make this area simply perfect for farmers. The main rivers here are the Godavari and the Krishna. These rivers make the soil in the area rich and fertile.

Gneiss is a rock that is created deep inside the earth through heat and immense pressure.

BLACK AND RED

The plateau region is called Rayalaseema and is made of something called gneiss. It has a river called the Penneru cutting through it. The plateau isn't smooth and flat; it has jagged ridges and valleys made of red and sometimes black soil.

THREE SEASONS MAKE A YEAR

Andhra Pradesh has three clear seasons: baking hot summers, mild winters and helpful monsoons. Farmers eagerly wait for the rain in July.

CROP SHOP

The farmers here grow plenty of rice, sugar cane, grains, pulses, cotton and groundnuts (among other things). There was a time when the rivers here were the only source of water for farmers. But a lot of effort was made to help get the river water into areas that had dams, canals and reservoirs too. Thanks to this, even the otherwise dry plateau is able to sustain agriculture.

The Nagarjuna Sagar Dam diverts the water from the Krishna and spreads it to many outlying farms.

HIDDEN WORDS

NAGARJUNA is such a big word. Mishki has been able to make ten smaller words from it. How many can you make?

TREE TRIUMPH

The coastal part of this state has many mangrove swamps. There are several dense forests too—especially along the slopes of the Eastern Ghats. These forests are full of teak, rosewood, bamboo and wild fruit trees. In other parts, there are neem, banyan, pipal and mango trees too!

Teak

Bamboo

Neem

WILD WONDERS

The forests of Andhra Pradesh boast some lovely wildlife. There are amazing animals here, like tigers, blackbuck, sloth bears, hyenas and chital—to name just a few! The birds are not to be left behind either. Pelicans, flamingoes and even the rare Jerdon's courser can be seen here. Oh! And you also find sea turtles in the shallow waters of the coast.

FUN FACTS

State Bird
Pala pitta
(Indian roller)

State Flower
White water lily

State Tree
Neem

State Animal
Jinka (Blackbuck)

WILDLIFE WORD GRID

Lots of Andhra Pradesh's wildlife is hidden in this grid. How many creatures can you spot? Remember to look from left to right and from top to bottom too!

I	U	H	Y	E	N	A	Y	T	R	E	W
T	P	A	L	A	P	I	T	T	A	S	A
U	E	D	B	L	A	C	K	B	U	C	K
R	L	F	G	H	J	J	I	N	K	A	B
T	I	G	E	R	A	K	L	Z	X	C	V
L	C	H	I	T	A	L	E	W	G	H	N
E	A	S	L	O	T	H	B	E	A	R	M
D	N	F	L	A	M	I	N	G	O	V	B

Jinka
Pala pitta
Tiger
Hyena
Chital
Pelican
Flamingo
Turtle
Blackbuck
Sloth bear

11

CITY CITY BANG BANG

AMARAVATI

This is a city that planners want to make super modern, with the best-ever infrastructure systems. It is slated to become Andhra Pradesh's capital in a few years.

VISAKHAPATNAM

Also known as Vizag, this is a busy port city and industrial hub. It is called the financial capital of Andhra Pradesh. It is also an important base for the Indian Navy.

VIJAYAWADA

This is a large city that sits on the banks of the Krishna River. There are many legends about how it got its name. One of them is that Goddess Durga killed a demon and then decided to rest here. The city, people say, is named after her victory (*vijaya* means 'victory').

TIRUPATI

This crowded city is best known for its temples, the largest being the Sri Venkateswara Temple. Millions of devotees flock here to pray, singing 'Govinda, Govinda'—a song of prayer to this temple's deity.

KADAPA

Once called Cuddapah, the name of this city means 'gateway' in Telugu—the local language. It was so named because one had to pass through this city to get to the Tirumala Hills. The black stone that is mined here is very popular, and it's used as flooring or for platforms in homes everywhere.

JUMBLED WORDS

Pushka wants to make sure he remembers everything. Can you help him unjumble the words?

Tirupati has a world famous _____ (MLETP).

The _____ (ONETS) found in Kadapa is black in colour.

The Indian _____ (VNYA) has a base in Vizag.

The Telugu word for victory is _____ (AJYAIV).

Amaravati is slated to become the _____ (PIACLTA) of Andhra Pradesh.

Long, long ago

Let's go back in time, Daadu. I am so curious about this state's history.

Well, we don't need a time machine for that. There are plenty of things in Andhra Pradesh that tell us all about its rich and colourful past. Come, let's find out more.

THOUSANDS OF YEARS AGO

In the earliest Sanskrit writings, almost back to 100 BCE, we can see the word 'Andhras' being mentioned to describe the people that lived in this region. But proper recorded history starts with the Mauryan dynasty, under Chandragupta Maurya.

BUDDHIST MESSENGERS

When Emperor Ashoka, the great Mauryan ruler, saw so much bloodshed, he gave up war and began to follow Buddhism. To spread Buddhism and the message of peace, he sent his messengers to the Andhra region. The Satavahanas, an important Andhra dynasty in power, accepted Buddhism.

SATAVAHANA SUCCESS

The Satavahanas were a powerful dynasty. They ruled over almost all of the Deccan Plateau. They supported different religions. They were also great lovers of art and architecture. Amaravati, their main city, had Buddhist architecture. During their rule, Buddhism grew, and they even set up a university to teach the Buddha's beliefs.

A great Buddhist teacher named Nagarjuna taught at the Nagarjunakonda University, which, though in ruins now, can still be visited today.

SAME TO SAME

Mishki is impressed with the Buddha's teachings. Can you help her find two identical pictures of Gautam Buddha?

A

B

C

D

E

F

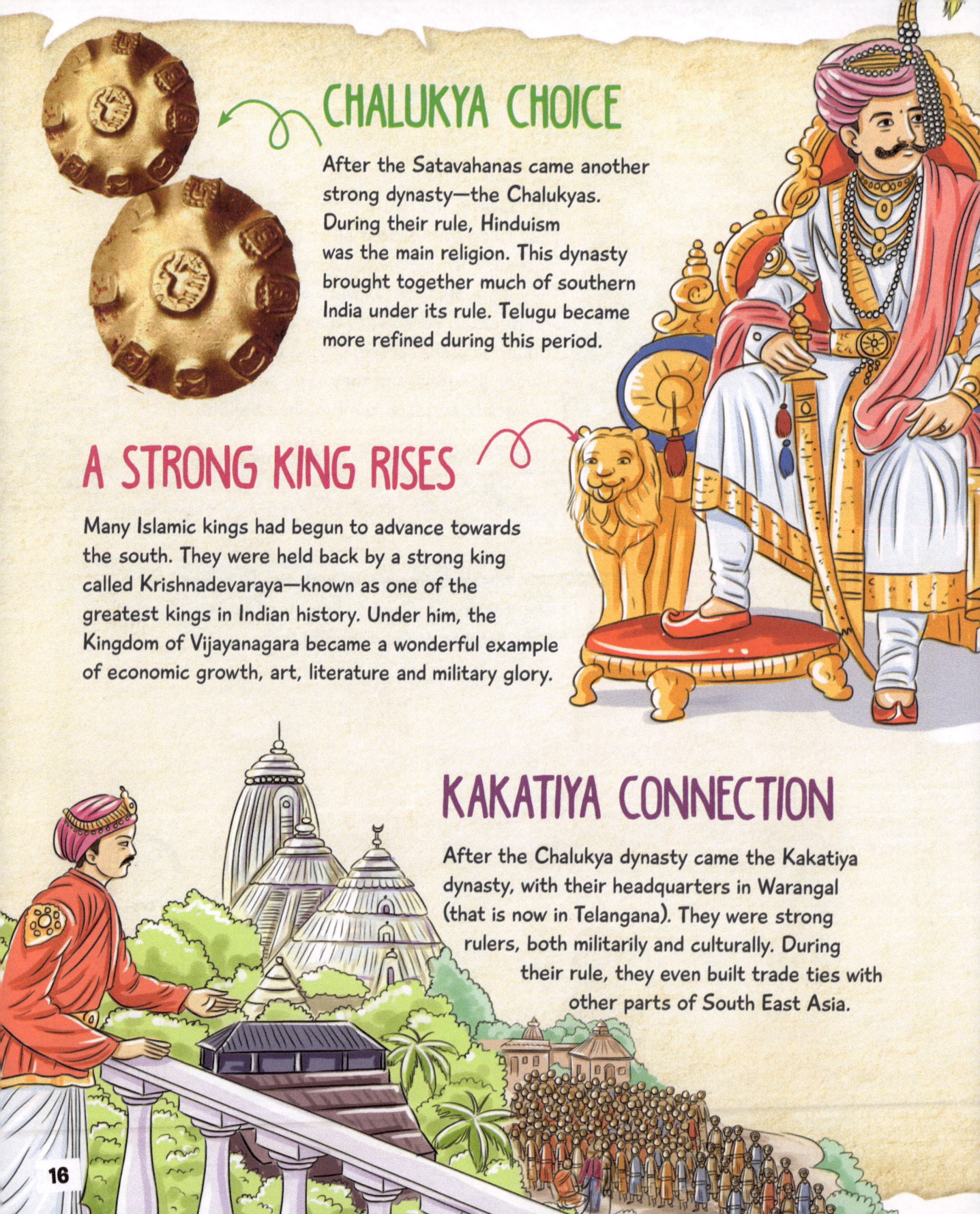

CHALUKYA CHOICE

After the Satavahanas came another strong dynasty—the Chalukyas. During their rule, Hinduism was the main religion. This dynasty brought together much of southern India under its rule. Telugu became more refined during this period.

A STRONG KING RISES

Many Islamic kings had begun to advance towards the south. They were held back by a strong king called Krishnadevaraya—known as one of the greatest kings in Indian history. Under him, the Kingdom of Vijayanagara became a wonderful example of economic growth, art, literature and military glory.

KAKATIYA CONNECTION

After the Chalukya dynasty came the Kakatiya dynasty, with their headquarters in Warangal (that is now in Telangana). They were strong rulers, both militarily and culturally. During their rule, they even built trade ties with other parts of South East Asia.

Coins tell us a lot about history.

SMALL DYNASTIES, BIG IMPACT

Many smaller dynasties had appeared in the northern and southern parts of India. The Bahmani Sultanate was one of these. The Qutb Shahi dynasty overcame the Vijayanagara Kingdom. They were progressive rulers and supported Telugu culture.

WHAT'S ODD?

In each of the rows below, there is one word that's odd. Can you find it?

CHALUKYA   SATAVAHANA   ROMAN

ASHOKA   KRISHNADEVARAYA   ABDUL KALAM

VIJAYANAGARA   TELANGANA   ANDHRA

DIFFERENT RULERS

The Andhra region was now under the rule of many smaller Nizams (as Muslim rulers were called), who were trying to assert themselves. Some of these Nizams took the support of European powers.

Did you know?
The unique culture of the Nizams is still evident in parts of Andhra Pradesh.

COLONIAL COUSINS

European traders—mainly the French and the British—had spotted India's potential. They were trying their best to gain control of the country. In exchange for their help, the Nizams gave the British a part of Andhra Pradesh. That is how so much of Andhra Pradesh came under British rule.

FIGHT FOR INDEPENDENCE

The British grew stronger and stronger, and they soon occupied all of India. They made rules that were unfair to the Indians, who protested—they wanted their independence back. Many leaders from Andhra Pradesh, like T. Prakasam Pantulu, fought hard. Finally, the British left India in 1947, giving back its independence.

A SEPARATE TELUGU SPEAKING STATE

During this time, Andhra Pradesh was a part of Tamilham (which also included Tamil Nadu and parts of Karnataka too). After Independence, it was decided that a part of Andhra Pradesh would be included in Madras state—and another part was made into Hyderabad state. But the original Andhras demanded their own state. And in 1956, Andhra Pradesh was born.

Now, Andhra Pradesh, Tamil Nadu and Karnataka each have their own language—though Telugu is common in both Andhra Pradesh and Telangana.

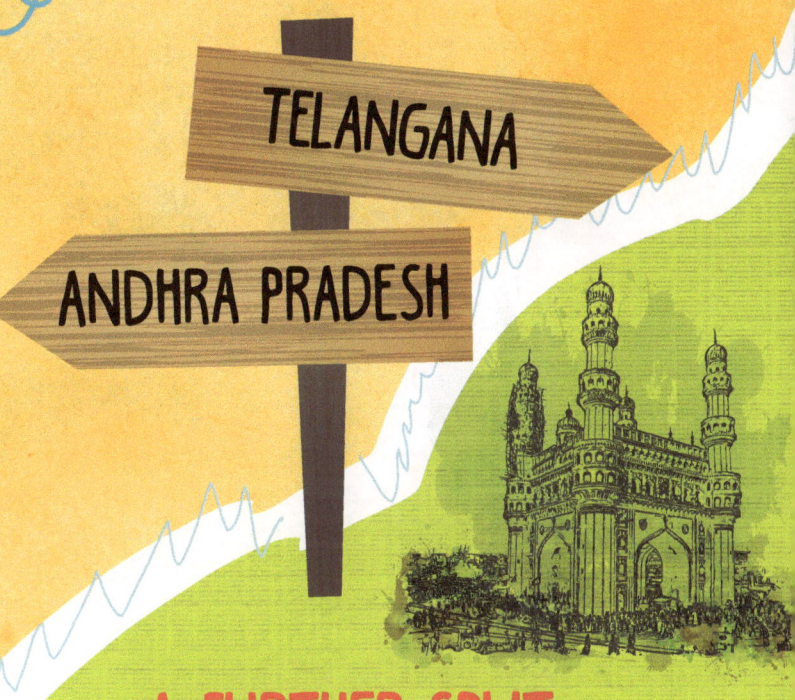

A FURTHER SPLIT

For many years, the state of Andhra Pradesh was a large one; Telangana was a part of it. But there were many people who wanted Telangana to have its own identity. In 2014, Telangana finally became a separate state. But after so many centuries of sharing a common history, the two states of Andhra Pradesh and Telangana still have many things they share, including culture, festivals and lifestyles.

Welcome
Susvaagatam

What is your name?
Mee peremiti?

Good morning
Shubhodayam

Goodbye
Vellostaanu

Do you speak Telugu?
Meeru Thelugu maatlaadathaaraa?

Hello
Namaskaram

My name is Mishki
Naa paeru Mishki

Good afternoon
Shubha dhina

MATCH THE WORDS

Pushka has already forgotten all his Telugu. Can you help him remember by matching the English phrases to their Telugu meanings?

Hello   Goodbye   Welcome   What is your name?   Good afternoon

Vellostaanu   Susvaagatam   Shubha dhina   Namaskaram   Mee peremiti?

21

A peep into their life

Come now, Daadu, let us meet some people. I want to learn all about how they live and what their culture is like.

Well, to start with, the people in this state are very cultured. And their culture is very diverse and interesting too. Let's take a look.

A POTPOURRI

People of many different religions live in this state, particularly Hindus and Muslims. Historically, because the Nizams ruled here for so long, Urdu is very much a part of the local language.

TRIBAL TRADITION

The famous Banjara tribe is said to have originated in this state, though they are now all over India. The Banjaras are colourful gypsies who have their own culture and tradition. In Andhra Pradesh, they are also called Sugadi or Lambadi.

A LITERARY TRADITION

Literature is very important here, and people are proud of the ancient Telugu literature from this state. It is said that thousands of years ago, a trio of poets named Nannaya, Tiranna and Errana translated the Mahabharata into Telugu. Other great poets included Yerrapragada and Pothana. The great King Krishnadevaraya was himself a great writer. So all these writings are an important part of Andhra Pradesh's cultural tradition.

The word 'Andhra' was first mentioned in an ancient Indian text called the Rig Veda.

ARTY STYLES

In ancient times, the artists of Andhra Pradesh were famous for their paintings. It is said that many of the paintings in the Ajanta Caves were created by these talented people. Even now, there are painters who keep this art alive. Some amazing styles are Cheriyal, Kalamkari and Nirmal.

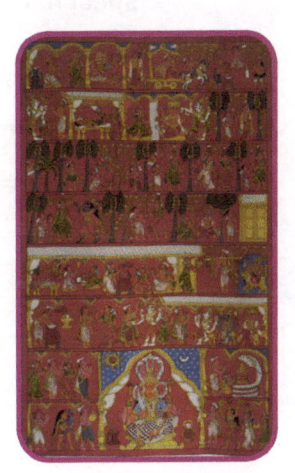

Cheriyal: Artists use rich colours to paint scenes from the epics on rolls of cloth. They even paint colourful masks.

Nirmal: These are mainly created by a community called the Nagash. The Mughals loved this art form and they encouraged artists who could do this.

Kalamkari: This is a century-old style of art. Paintings are made by dipping bamboo sticks in vegetable dyes. Artists create lovely designs of flowers, animals and gods.

DANCE, DANCE, DANCE

There are many, many dance forms here—both classical as well as folk. Let's discover some!

BUTTA BOMMALU

This is an entertaining dance in which the dancers wear masks representing different characters. The movements are subtle but great fun to watch.

KUCHIPUDI

This lovely classical dance is a beautiful mix of song, speech, dance, expressions and gestures. It is named after the village of Kuchipudi, where this dance form probably originated.

DAPPU

Dancers wear costumes and dance to the beat of cymbals and drums, all while telling stories from the epics.

VEERANATYAM

This translates to 'the dance of the brave'. This energetic dance is based on a legend that says Lord Shiva was furious when his wife Sati (people say she was later reborn as Parvati) died. He danced this dance in great fury.

TAPPETA GULLU

This is a vigorous dance that men perform to make the rain gods happy.

BONALU

Performers of this dance skilfully balance a pot on their head while dancing. This is done to praise Mahankali, a village deity.

RHYME TIME

Mishki is busy writing a poem about the dances she has seen. She needs two words to rhyme with each word given. Can you help her?

Rain _____ _____

Pots _____ _____

Folk _____ _____

Mask _____ _____

FESTIVAL FUN

Time to celebrate! Let's have some festival fun the way people do in Andhra Pradesh.

NEW YEAR JOY

Ugadi is the Telugu New Year. But it isn't in January—it's usually in March, April or May. Front doors are decorated with mango leaves to welcome the new year. People like to cook a sweet dish called bhakshya.

TIRUPATI GANGA JATARA

Tirupati has loads of festivals. The Ganga Jatara is one during which devotees pray to Gangamma, the guardian goddess. Legend goes that in the old days, there were some rulers who were cruel to women. Gangamma destroyed them. People now celebrate Gangamma's victory over evil.

GOWRI HABBA

At the centre of this celebration is Gowri (Lord Shiva's wife and Lord Ganesha's mother). They say that the day this festival is celebrated is when Lord Ganesha came to take his mother back home to his father, from her parents' home. Women dress up idols of Gowri and pray to her for strength and peace.

PONGAL

This harvest festival is a lot of fun. Farmers thank Mother Nature for giving them a good harvest. They make much of their cattle as well. For four days, they pray and celebrate. Of course, yummy food isn't too far. Every house makes a delicious, sweet rice dish called pongal.

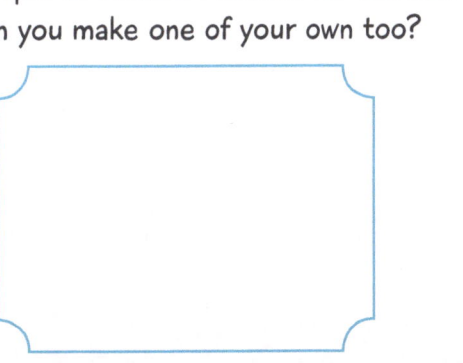

HAPPY NEW YEAR

Mishki and Pushka want to wish the people of Andhra Pradesh for the new year. They have made a lovely card. Can you make one of your own too?

27

HANDY HANDICRAFT

Andhra Pradesh has always been home to super creative people. No wonder their handicrafts are so amazing. Let's see what kind of wonderful things they make here.

TOY TOWN

Kondapalli is a famous town full of toymakers. The wooden toys made here are called Kondapalli *bommalu*. Artists paint these toys in brilliant colours. You'll see amazing miniature figures of gods, bridal couples, animals and dolls. Oh, these toys are collectors' items, all right!

TOY PLOY

A kind of softwood called Tella Poniki is used to make these unusual toys, which are also called *dapalli* toys. These are made by mixing tamarind powder, sawdust, water colours and enamel gum. Craftsmen have been making these for centuries. The little toys are usually either idols of gods or household characters (like people cooking or milking cows). How sweet!

HEAVY METAL

Bidri art is said to have originated in Hyderabad. Craftsmen use a sharp chisel to engrave patterns on metal. Then, with a hammer, they insert silver wires in these indentations. They make things like boxes, lamps and paper cutters. What skill!

SHARP AS A NEEDLE

Banjara needlecraft was born among wanderers and nomadic people. They made the most intricate and beautiful designs with their embroidery. Now people use it on their furniture and clothes too!

SHADOW PLAY

Pushka has carved a wooden toy, just like the craftsmen of Andhra Pradesh do. Can you find its shadow?

Bricks and stones

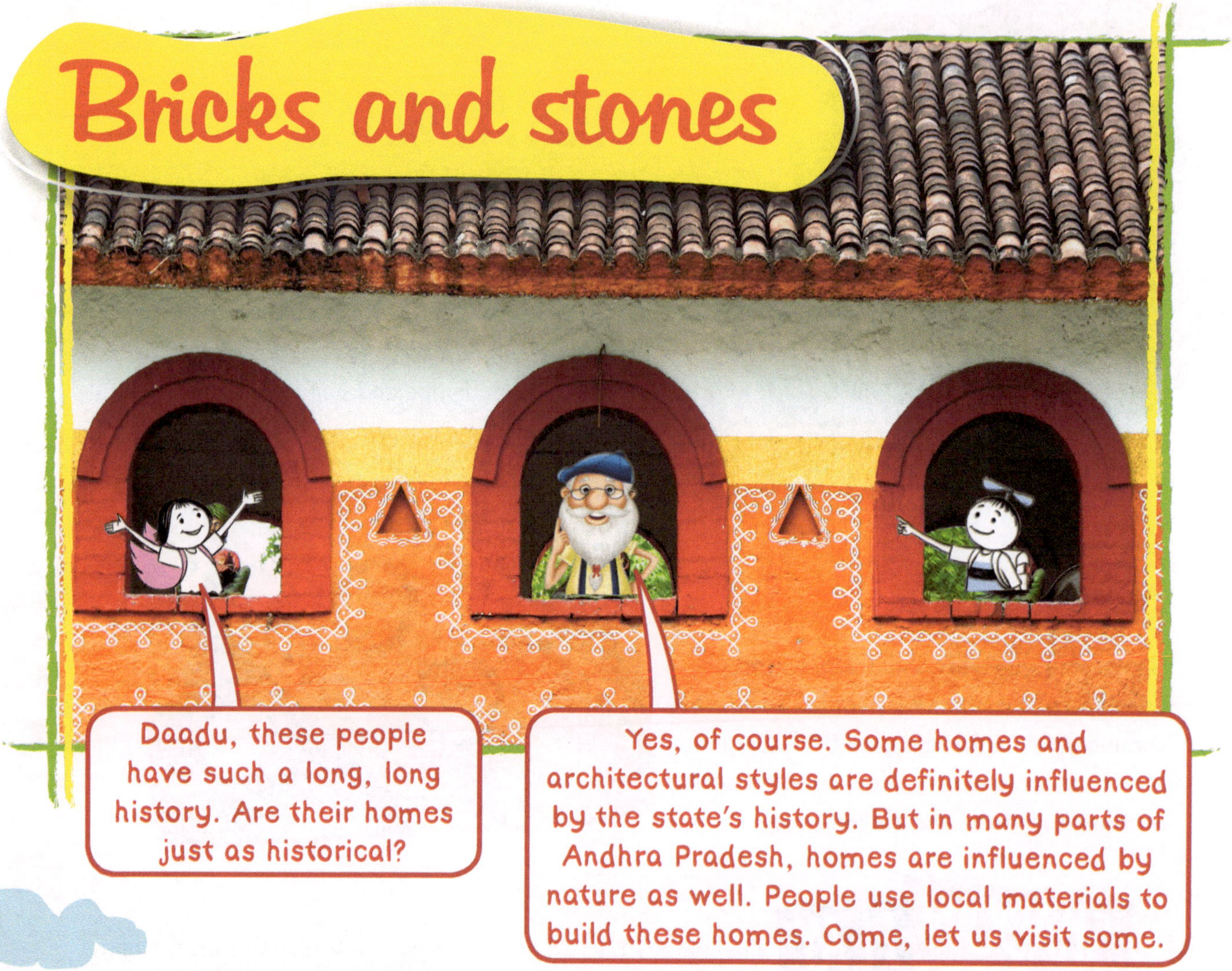

> Daadu, these people have such a long, long history. Are their homes just as historical?

> Yes, of course. Some homes and architectural styles are definitely influenced by the state's history. But in many parts of Andhra Pradesh, homes are influenced by nature as well. People use local materials to build these homes. Come, let us visit some.

CHUTTILLU HOMES

In Telugu, *chuttillu* means 'round house'. Chuttillu houses are built along the coast, where cyclones can take place. People build homes close to each other for safety, so that they can stay sheltered during fierce winds. These houses are built in concentric circles. The year's food supplies are kept in the innermost room. How interesting!

These homes are similar to the homes in neighbouring states, like Tamil Nadu and Karnataka, because these were all one large state in the past.

VILLAGE WONDERS

In villages, where most of the people are farmers, people build their homes with materials that are available to them. They construct simple mud huts with thatched roofs. Cows and buffaloes are important to the family, and there are separate spaces for them that the family also uses to store extra produce from time to time.

ROYAL TOUCH

Influenced by the royal style of the Nizams who lived in this region, many wealthy Muslim families build their homes to have intricate screens, arches, fountains and courtyards—all making these homes almost palatial.

HOME SWEET HOME

Pushka and Mishki are building a house. But they have lost their key! Can you help them find it?

Standing strong

Daadu, I see so many different types of historical buildings. Can we go and visit all of them?

We won't have time to see them all, Pushka, because there are thousands of amazing temples, forts, palaces and monuments. But if you hurry, we can see some of the most beautiful ones. So come along! Let's get started right away.

TEMPLE BELLS

There are literally thousands of temples across Andhra Pradesh—both big and small—that devotees throng to all year round. Some of these are architectural masterpieces, while some are simple structures. Either way, they are very important to people.

TIRUMALA TEMPLE AT TIRUPATI

This world-famous temple is among the most important in Andhra Pradesh. It is also called the Temple of Seven Hills, because it sits majestically on top of one of seven important peaks in the area. The main deity is Lord Venkateswara (also known as Balaji). The temple has a long history too! King Krishnadevaraya donated a lot of his fortune, with which the temple was enhanced. Over the years, many kings came here to pray.

Tiru means 'holy' or 'sacred' and *mala* means 'mountain'. So Tirumala literally means 'holy mountains'.

WHAT'S DIFFERENT?

Mishki and Pushka have drawn a picture of the idol of Lord Balaji. But there are ten differences between the two pictures they have drawn. Can you find the differences?

SRIKALAHASTI TEMPLE

This lovely temple is more than 2000 years old. People call it 'Kailas of the South' because it is a Shiva temple and Lord Shiva lived on Mount Kailas. There is a lovely story behind how this temple got its name. Legend goes that a spider (*sri*), a serpent (*kala*) and an elephant (*hasti*) worshipped Lord Shiva devoutly. The temple is an architectural wonder.

AHOBILAM

This beautiful temple has a legend behind it. It is said that it was here that Lord Narasimha (who is supposed to be an incarnation of Lord Vishnu) slayed the evil demon Hiranyakashipu. He then appeared to bless his son, Prahlad, who was his devotee.

KANAKA DURGA TEMPLE

This temple is situated on a hill on the banks of the Krishna. The view from here is stunning. The main goddess here is Durga. During Dussehra, there is a big event, where thousands come to celebrate and pray.

MALLIKARJUNA JYOTIRLINGA

Here's an interesting legend. People believe that it was here that Lord Shiva's sacred bull prayed so hard that Lord Shiva and his wife Parvati appeared here to bless the bull. A massive fort surrounds this temple and people from all religions come here to pray.

CRACK THE CODE

Pushka and Mishki have formed a secret society. To join their society, you must know their made-up password. Can you crack the code and figure out the password?

1 = A	2 = N	3 = R	4 = M	5 = H	6 = S
7 = I	8 = L	9 = O	10 = D		

8 9 3 10   2 1 3 1 6 7 4 5 1

☐ ☐ ☐ ☐ ☐ ☐ ☐ ☐ ☐ ☐ ☐ ☐ ☐

FORTIFIED

There are lots of historical forts in Andhra Pradesh. Not surprising, because the state has had so many kings and wars over the centuries.

PENUKONDA FORT

This fort was important in the Vijayanagara Empire. There are some lovely structures inside. The Gagan Mahal (Sky Palace) was a summer resort. There's a shrine called the Babayya Darga, which shows how people of different religions happily lived together in those ancient days.

CHANDRAGIRI FORT

Chandragiri was once the capital city of the Vijayanagara Empire. Chandragiri Fort has a moat around it. It has a delightful palace inside it too! Nowadays, the palace is lit up at night and looks like it belongs in a fairy tale.

GOOTY FORT

This fort is one of the oldest in Andhra Pradesh. Many kings have attacked and conquered it over the centuries—including the Marathas, Haider Ali and, finally, the British. It's said to have a shell-like shape and the view from here is amazing.

CROSSWORD TIME

Help Mishki and Pushka solve this crossword and remember all that they have seen!

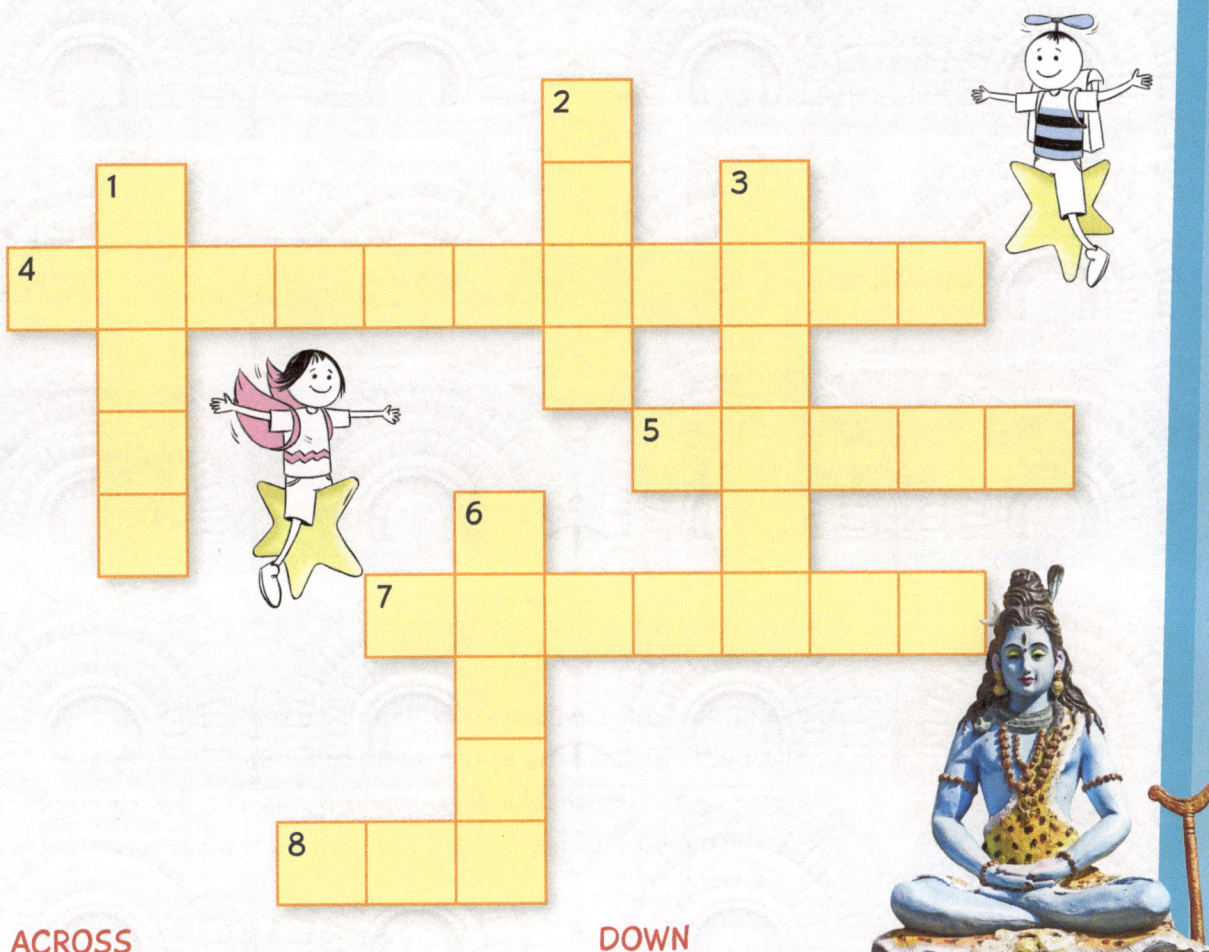

ACROSS

4. The lovely fort that was once in the capital city of the Vijayanagara Empire.

5. The shape of Gooty Fort.

7. King Krishnadevaraya donated a lot of his _____ to a temple.

8. Gagan Mahal means _____ Palace.

DOWN

1. The god who has a sacred bull.

2. It surrounds the fort so enemies can't get in.

3. Of whom Lord Narasimha is a reincarnation.

6. This fort was captured by the Marathas, Hyder Ali and the British.

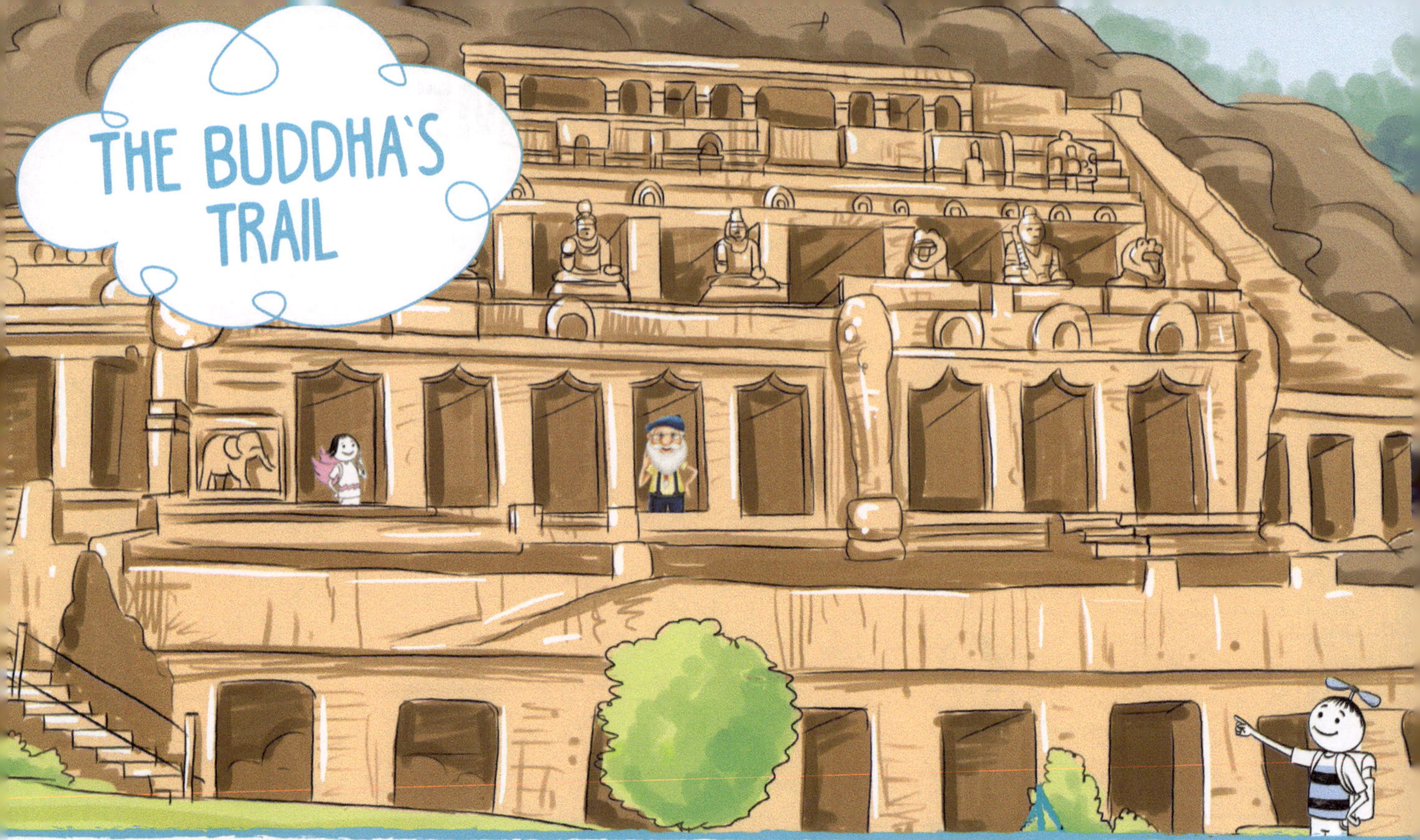

THE BUDDHA'S TRAIL

UNDAVALLI CAVES

These mysterious caves are cut deep into rocks high on a hillside by the river Krishna. The caves seem to be dedicated to the deities Anantapadmanabha Swamy and Narasimha Swamy. Buddhist monks also meditated or rested here during their travels.

BOJJANNAKONDA

One day, a British archaeologist discovered something amazing—a 2000-year-old Buddhist complex, full of rock-cut caves, clay tablets with inscriptions, coins and many beautiful stupas. It's hard to believe that this kind of beauty was created so many thousands of years ago.

GUNTUPALLI CAVES

These caves are said to be among the most famous Buddhist sites around here. Perched on a hill, there are rock-cut images of the Buddha, stupas and inscriptions that are hundreds of years old.

People say that a great Buddhist scholar called Dignaga stayed here for a while.

NAGARJUNAKONDA

This is actually a historical Buddhist town, where the great Buddhist scholar Acharya Nagarjuna lived thousands of years ago. When people dug deeper, they found an entire town, complete with a university, royal baths, marble sculptures and carvings. Must have been an amazing place!

Working hard

What do the people of Andhra Pradesh do for a living, Daadu?

The people here are clever and hard-working too. They have many different occupations. Come, let's have a look.

FARMER, FARMER, WHAT DO YOU GROW?

A large number of people in Andhra Pradesh are farmers. Many of them grow rice, which is the staple food of the people who live here. But that's not all! They also grow sugar cane, tobacco, maize, pulses and several other crops.

Andhra Pradesh is one of the largest producers of shrimp in India.

SOMETHING FISHY

As this state has such a long coastline, people living along the coast love fish. This is why fishing is an important occupation. Aquaculture (the breeding of fish) is a big business.

WOODY WOOD

The woodlands of this state are lush and plentiful. They give the people timber, teak and eucalyptus. A lot of people are busy converting this wood into products like oil, furniture, gum, medicines and tobacco.

ANIMAL FARM

There are a whole lot of farmers who raise animals. This is called animal husbandry. Sheep, goats, poultry, water buffaloes—these are the main animals that are bred for dairy and egg production. Dairy farming is a big profession here.

FARM FRESH

Pushka has decided to work on a farm. Can you circle all the animals he will see there?

SERVICE WITH A SMILE

The service industry is really big in Andhra Pradesh. This means that there are a lot of people who work in banks, communication companies and tourism; all of them serve their customers. These people typically work in offices.

TECH GENIUSES

The IT (information technology) industry in Andhra Pradesh is very advanced. A large number of hardware and software engineers come from this state. They don't just work in Andhra Pradesh—they take their skills with them to other states and countries as well.

HANDY HANDLOOMS

Andhra Pradesh is famous for its wonderful handlooms and skilled weavers. The saris that are made here are very popular. These sari weaves have lovely names, like Pochampalli, Venkatagiri and Narayanpet. Many of these are named after the village they have come from.

TOY TRADITION

There are many traditional toymakers here, who craft the most delightful wooden toys. Some of these simple figures are shaped like the objects that people found during the excavations of many sites of the Indus Valley Civilization.

PATTERN PERFECT

Mishki wants to draw an ikat pattern. Can you help her copy the one shown here?

Ikat is a style of weaving that is unique and much loved. People make clothes, saris and furnishings with this lovely geometric-patterned weave.

Yum yum yum

Well, first I'll tell you a little bit about the different kinds of food. Then you can decide what you want to eat. Does that sound good?

At last, we have reached my favourite part. I've been smelling the most delicious aromas. What's the plan for food, Daadu?

FOOD WITH A HISTORY

Even the food in this state has been influenced by history. Both the Nizams who lived here and the rajas have influenced the food. So you will find two distinct kinds of cuisine.

VEGGIE WONDERS

There are many vegetarians in this state. And the food can be super spicy! Red and green chillies add the spice, tamarind makes it tangy and coconut mellows the taste.

PERFECT PULIHORA

This spicy rice dish has loads of tamarind. In fact, the word *puli* means 'sour' and *hora* means 'food'.

Tangy Treat

ANDHRA PAPPU

Pappu means 'dal' in Telugu. There are many kinds of yummy pappus, made with tomato and tamarind. They taste wonderful with rice.

SNACK TIME

Andhra Pradesh loves its snacks. There are some delicious snacks here, like chekkalu, guggillu, bondalu and mirapakaya bajji. They may be hard to pronounce if you don't speak Telugu, but they are wonderfully tasty to eat.

GONGURA STYLE

Gongura is a leaf that is very flavourful. People in Andhra Pradesh use it to make all kinds of delicious dishes. You will find chutneys, curries and meat dishes that use this leaf.

EAT LIKE A NIZAM

The Nizams of Hyderabad loved their food, all right. Their chefs laboured over their cooking, and you will see that this kind of food is slow-cooked for hours to get it just right.

BIRYANI BONANZA

The biryani from this state is famous across the world. Eat the traditional biryani in Hyderabad and you feel like you are transported into a royal dining room. Meat, saffron, dry fruits and the best quality of rice all come together to make this amazing dish.

KEBAB CORNER

The Nizams loved their kebabs. Meltingly delicious meat kebabs are made here. There are lots of different types—like boti kebab, shish kebab and kalmi kebab.

DALCHA DELIGHT

This is a thick gravy-like dish that is made with either meat or pumpkin and enjoyed with rice.

SWEET TOOTH

The sweet dishes of Andhra Pradesh are really special!

SHEER KHURMA

This is a yummy vermicelli pudding that tastes heavenly.

SHAHI TUKDA

Shahi means 'royal' and *tukda* means 'piece'. This dish is made up of slices of fried bread in a sinful sugar syrup.

FOODIE MAZE

Mishki, Pushka and Daadu Dolma have each chosen what they want to eat. Can you help them get to their chosen dish?

POOTHAREKULU

This is made with layers of rice batter and sugar or jaggery. It's as thin as paper. Making this dish is hard work, but it's worth it.

What to wear?

I'm stuffed, Daadu. I want to wear something loose and comfy and have a snooze.

Well then, come and see what clothes you will get to wear in Andhra Pradesh.

NAWAABI STYLE

Muslim women often wear magnificent salwar kameezes or shararas (flared trousers). Many wear a burka in public. Men wear sherwanis for special occasions. On normal days, they wear kurta-pyjamas and sometimes a fez, which is a type of hat.

A fez

TRIBAL SPLENDOUR

Tribal women wear a colourful skirt called a ghaghra with a blouse called a choli. They also wear a lot of silver jewellery. Visitors and tourists love to buy this chunky jewellery.

DAPPER DHOTIS

Traditionally, Hindu men wore a dhoti and a kurta. Now, that has given way to modern attire, like jeans and T-shirts. But many men still prefer the comfort of a dhoti.

VERY SARI

Many women in Andhra Pradesh wear saris. They have such a lot of choice too, because there are wonderful traditional weaves they can choose from.

Autograph, please?

Are all the famous people in Andhra Pradesh kings and queens?

Oh no, not at all! There are many others who have played an important part in the state. Some of them are not alive anymore, but they are just as important. Let's meet some of them now.

NANNAYA

He was one of the earliest Telugu writers and started writing the Mahabharata in Telugu.

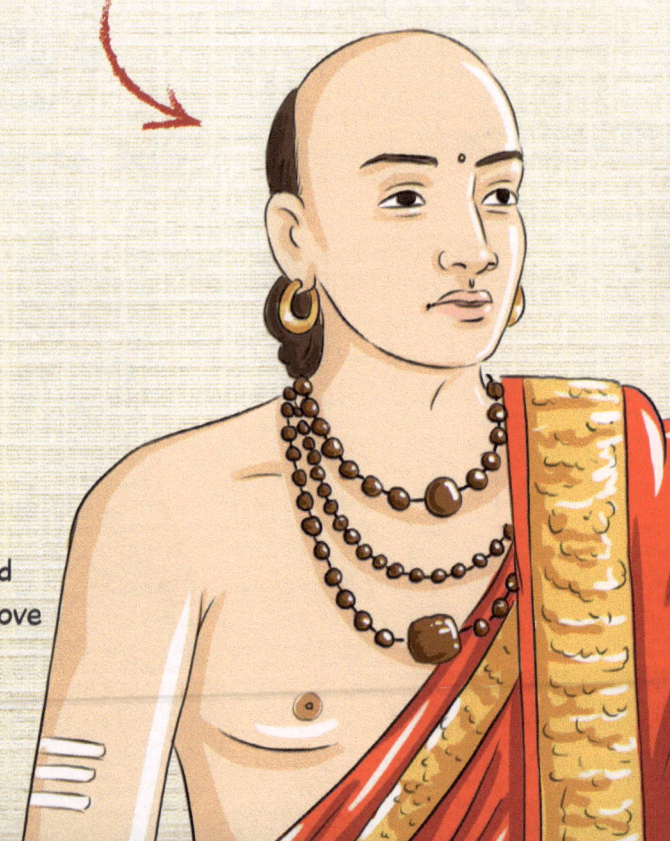

GONA BUDDA REDDY

He was a great poet, also known as Ranganatha, who wrote a treatise on the Ramayana. It is called *Ranganatha Ramayanam*. People from this state love it and recite it during puppet shows and cultural events, even after so many thousands of years.

JIDDU KRISHNAMURTI

He was a philosopher, writer and speaker, who wrote about human relationships, meditation and theosophy. He tried to bring about social change through his writing.

C.K. NAYUDU

He was a great cricketer and the first captain of the Indian Test match team. He played many matches for India.

N.T. RAMA RAO

Nandamuri Taraka Rama Rao, or simply NTR, was one of Andhra Pradesh's most iconic figures. He was an actor, director, politician and editor all rolled into one. He was the chief minister of Andhra Pradesh for many years. People affectionately called him Anna— meaning 'brother'.

RAJA AND RADHA REDDY

This talented couple are famous Kuchipudi dancers. They have made this dance known across the world. They have won many awards, including the Padma Shri and Padma Bhushan.

KALLAM ANJI REDDY

He was the entrepreneur who founded Dr Reddy's Laboratories, one of India's largest pharmaceutical companies. He also did a lot of social work for the upliftment of the underprivileged. He has been awarded both the Padma Shri and Padma Bhushan.

KARNAM MALLESWARI

She is a weightlifter and the first Indian woman to win an Olympic medal.

PRABHAS

Born Prabhas Raju Uppalapati, he is the actor who played the role of Baahubali in two of the highest-grossing Indian films of all time.

CHIRANJEEVI

This famous actor's real name is Konidela Siva Sankara Vara Prasad. He's a movie star, dancer, producer, singer, politician and businessman.

S.P. BALASUBRAHMANYAM

He is a singer, actor, music director and film producer, who is reportedly featured in the Guinness Book of World Records for having sung more songs than anyone else in the world.

MATCH THE MASTERS

Can you match the people to their professions or what they are known for?

Karnam Malleswari	Dancers
Raja and Radha Reddy	Cricketer
Prabhas	Philosopher
Jiddu Krishnamurti	Singer
C.K. Nayudu	Actor
S.P. Balasubrahmanyam	Weightlifter

Once upon a time . . .

Daadu, I'm sleepy now. Will you tell us a story from Andhra Pradesh? I'd love to listen to one before I sleep.

Well then, settle down. I have a lovely story from this amazing state.

THE BOY WHO COULD UNDERSTAND ANIMALS

In a little village in Andhra Pradesh, there lived a young boy called Narayan. He lived with his parents in a tiny hut near the forest. The family didn't have too much money, but they were good-hearted people and happy with whatever they had.

Narayan spent a lot of time in the forests near his home. He brought home wood and berries, and the family made do with that. He was friends with all the animals, even the ones whom most people were afraid of. In fact, two snakes who lived in a burrow near Narayan's house were very good friends of his.

Narayan would play with them fearlessly, for they didn't harm people who didn't harm them. He was gentle and loving with them, and they loved him back.

One morning, Narayan walked into the forest. His snake friends were nowhere to be seen.

'Oh, my snake friends, where are you?' Narayan called out. Suddenly, he heard a rustling sound. He followed the sound and found, to his horror, that his snake friends were trapped in a net that some hunter had laid out. Narayan ran forward and quickly cut the ropes of the net, setting the snakes free.

That night, as Narayan slept, he had a dream. Nag Devta, the king of all snakes, appeared before him.

'Narayan, you are good boy,' the snake god said. 'You have saved two snakes from being killed. I will reward you with whatever you desire. What do you want?'

'Oh, Nag Devta,' replied Narayan, 'I am happy with what I have. I have my animal friends and my parents. I wish for nothing more.'

Nag Devta was pleased with Narayan's reply.

'I shall bless you. From now on, you will be able to understand everything that any animal says.' Saying so, the snake god disappeared.

The next morning, Narayan woke up, confused about his dream. But he soon forgot all about it. When he went to the forest, he found that he could understand everything that the animals said. He understood all that the birds sang about and when the animals asked for help. He was ecstatic! He began to spend more time than ever with his beloved animals.

One day, his father fell very ill. The family was in trouble. They didn't have much money. Narayan decided to go to the city and ask the king for help.

On the way there, he heard some parrots talking. 'The king's granary is going to be empty soon. That means there will be a famine,' one parrot said to another. Narayan was horrified. He decided to warn the king and, upon reaching his court, asked to be taken to him.

'Your Majesty, I came to ask for help. But I think it is you who will need help,' he said, bowing deeply.

'What do you mean I will need help?' thundered the king. 'Arrest this cheeky youth at once!'

'Your Majesty, your granary is going to be empty. And soon, there will be a famine,' explained Narayan.

'How do you know that? Have you visited my granary?' questioned the king sarcastically. No one was allowed in the granary without escort.

'I heard some parrots talking,' said Narayan.

'Hah! You expect me to believe that you understand what parrots say?' the king exploded. But he sent someone to the granary to check. To his amazement, the granary really was on the verge of being empty.

The king realized at once that this boy was special. He immediately appointed Narayan minister and sent the best doctors to treat Narayan's father. Narayan and his family were never in need of anything ever again.

TRAVEL DIARY

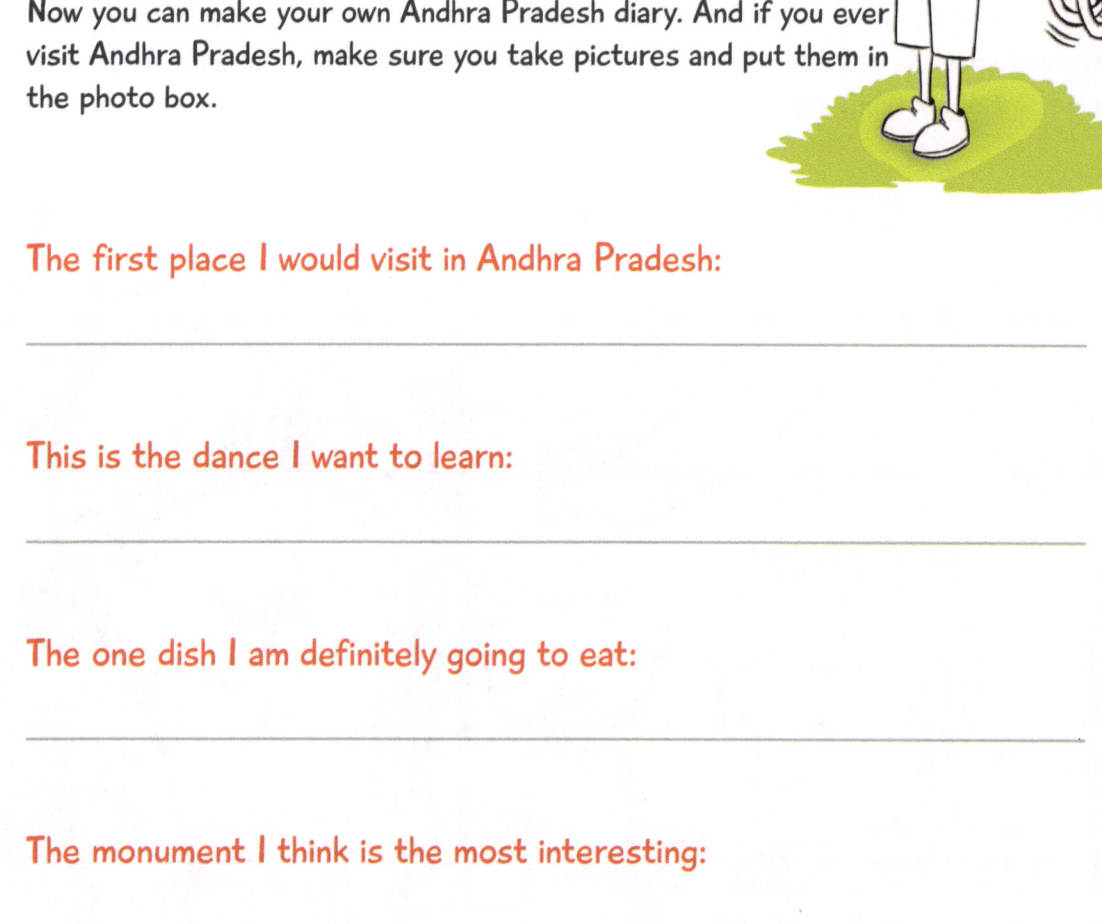

Have you enjoyed this trip to Andhra Pradesh with your friends Mishki and Pushka—and, of course, with Daadu Dolma?

Now you can make your own Andhra Pradesh diary. And if you ever visit Andhra Pradesh, make sure you take pictures and put them in the photo box.

The first place I would visit in Andhra Pradesh:

_____

This is the dance I want to learn:

_____

The one dish I am definitely going to eat:

_____

The monument I think is the most interesting:

_____

The one famous person from Andhra Pradesh I would love to meet:

_____

The most interesting historical character from Andhra Pradesh is:

_____

The festival from Andhra Pradesh that I think is the most fun:

_____

The five words that I think describe Andhra Pradesh the best are:

_____

_____

_____

_____

_____

My Andhra Pradesh memories:

ANSWERS

page 9 HIDDEN WORDS

Here are some words you can form: gun, jar, nag, nun, rag, ran, rug, urn, rang, rung, jaguar

page 11 WILDLIFE WORD GRID

page 13 JUMBLED WORDS

TEMPLE, STONE, NAVY, VIJAY, CAPITAL

page 15 SAME TO SAME

B and F are alike.

page 17 WHAT'S ODD

ROMAN, ABDUL KALAM, VIJAYANAGARA

page 21 MATCH THE WORDS

Hello—Namaskaram; Goodbye—Vellostaanu; Welcome—Susvaagatam; What is your name?—Mee peremiti?; Good afternoon—Shubha dhina

page 25 RHYME TIME

Here are some rhyming words: brain, chain, dots, spots, joke, poke, ask, flask

page 29 SHADOW PLAY

page 31 HOME SWEET HOME

page 33 WHAT'S DIFFERENT?

page 35 CRACK THE CODE

LORD NARASIMHA

page 37 CROSSWORD TIME

page 41 FARM FRESH

page 47 FOODIE MAZE

page 53 MATCH THE MASTERS

Karnam Malleswari—Weightlifter; Raja and Radha Reddy—Dancers; Prabhas—Actor; Jiddu Krishnamurti—Philosopher; C.K. Nayudu—Cricketer; S.P. Balasubrahmanyam—Singer